THE FIELD DOES NOT COME TO THE FARMER

A Pocket Guide to Organizational Leadership for Gen Y & Z

JEREMIAH SINKS

Copyright © 2020 Jeremiah Sinks

All rights reserved.

DEDICATION

This book is dedicated to my children.
I have always been, I am, and I shall always be, immensely
proud of you.

CONTENTS

　　　　Introduction　　　　　　　　　　　i

1　The Importance of Needs and Wants in Generations

2　Connecting With Gen Y & Z

3　Your Team's Performance is a Direct Reflection of Your Performance as a Leader

4　Leadership Behavior Dictates Culture

5　Total Rewards with an Emphasis on Intrinsic & Extrinsic Values for Gen Y & Z

6　Treat this as a Process

7　Epilogue

8　Bibliography

9　Acknowledgements

10　About the Author

INTRODUCTION

Far too many organizations are over-managed and under-led. There is a massive difference between Leading and Managing.

To be world class, we need to be both good managers and leaders. Managing is for processes. We need continuity, stability and predictability from our processes therefore we need to have good systems in place. When it comes to people though, we do not like being managed. We want to be led.

Management is for processes. Leadership is for people.

When we fail to recognize this, we end up trying to manage people through ever-increasingly complex systems and system tools that ultimately do not move the needle in the right direction and actually, instead, create a toxic perception of the organization.

When we are managers and not leaders, people tend to view us as a "Boss." Let me describe a "boss" so as we move forward, when I use that word it makes sense to you what I mean.

I can hire a boss right off the street in five minutes; no special skills needed other than the willingness to try and catch people doing the wrong thing and when they do, they break out the management tools (written coaching, discipline, etc.). A boss just needs to be willing to bark, growl and occasionally bite.

A boss tries to chase people into place and push people to get things done. Think to yourself for a moment about the worst person you ever worked for in your life. When I use the word boss, it is that person in your mind.

You can spot bosses in the workplace fairly easily. Simply watch when a boss enters the work area of their people. Notice what the people tend to do? Scatter if possible…" tighten up" if they aren't fast enough to scatter…

If we understand that's what happens when a boss enters

the work area, then we must understand what happens when a boss leaves the work area…what do those people now do?

Do they do the right thing when no one is looking? With a boss, that answer varies widely. This is why bosses struggle to take a day off, or a vacation. They tend to create an atmosphere that is so heavily dependent on them constantly policing and barking that when they leave, their team's performance dips.

The next natural question is then what is a "leader?"

A leader is someone who gets the willing participation of others to follow a vision. Willing participation…those are two powerful words in that definition. When a leader hits the work area, you don't see people tighten up and scatter. We are all on the same team pursuing the same goals. The Team takes care of the Team.

Let me now plant a foundational seed for you, the reader. Think about your current organization and consider what you "make."

For many of us, our initial response is our product whether that's a physical product or a service…and that is not accurate. This topic is leadership; therefore, what you, as a leader, make are people and history. Those two things in turn work in the background to create your career legacy as a leader. What will people who work with you remember ten years from now, the products or the people? We must also understand that this legacy of yours is going to be; whether you've considered it or not. Therefore, you may as well do it with intent and create a legacy you are proud of instead of getting whatever you get because you didn't steer it. Either way, it shall exist.

Imagine if a Farmer tried to be successful the way many managers try to be successful: stand around in my office surrounded by my policies and procedures and blaming people when they don't yield what I want. The farmer may be pictured standing on their porch yelling at the crops to grow because he bought the seed and planted the seed and

The Field Does Not Come to the Farmer

all the books say seeds are supposed to grow.
We'd all starve.
In order to harvest, we have to meet the need where it is,
then cultivate it to where we want it to be.

1 THE IMPORTANCE OF NEEDS AND WANTS IN GENERATIONS

Let's consider some generations and their general traits & characteristics.

We'll start with the Silent Generation, or Traditionalists as they are also called. These are folks whom were born before 1946 by most definitions. When we consider the common characteristics of these folks, they tend to be very hard working, very thrifty, they do not complain (even when they have reason to!), they are self-sacrificing. They historically have done what needed done, even against exceedingly difficult backdrops.

If I ask you to consider why that generation is commonly like that, you might say things such as the great Depression; and World War's. I would agree; and where that leads us to is that summarily, they are the way they are based on their formative years. What they experienced as they were growing up shaped, to a large part, the way they are as adults. As a young man I washed dishes in a nursing home while in high school and I spoke to many older folks. Their experiences are simply astonishing. Sending children to work. Eating popcorn for breakfast and dinner.

What they went through will never not be astonishing.

Let's then consider the next generation after them, the Baby Boomers. Baby Boomers tended to value different things such as vacations, having a car, pursuing further education, having adventures. It was very important to them to be successful. Typically, this was defined by monetary related items which meant pursuing job titles, pay, overtime...they were the original "workaholics" as they pursued these things. It was very important to them.

Why are the Baby Boomers so different in their general traits than the Traditionalists? It is the same answer as before: primarily due to their formative years. Summarily- Baby Boomers stood on the shoulders of the generation before them. The traditionalists raised their children with the intent to give them a better life than they had. Therefore, due to the efforts and intent of their parents- Baby Boomers had higher expectations. Don't go to work as a child, get your education. Go to college. Enjoy the rewards of hard work rather than simply surviving. Thrive.

The linkage in the example of Traditionalists and Baby Boomers is critical to understand. As parents we naturally want our kids to have it better than we did. Over time, that definition of better means many different things...with one exception. It always means, one way or another, "have higher expectations than we did." Always.

Why is this linkage critical to understand? Because this linkage exists as we continue to step through generation after generation. After the Baby Boomers, Gen X had different characteristics, traits and values. I am Gen X. I did not want to be a workaholic, for me it was very important to have more of a work/life balance than the Baby Boomers. As Gen X, our formative years taught us lessons about the good and bad examples of the prior generation and we sharpened and shaped our core values...as every generation does.

After Gen X came the echo Boomers, or Millennials or Gen Y. Now Gen Z is entering the workforce as well. Where am I going with this? Succinctly to this point: I hear a lot of frustrated hiring managers, supervisors, etc. say things like "these kids are lazy, entitled, soft...", insert your own narrative that you've heard. We've all heard it. Folks, it is a myth. It is incorrect. It is simply not true and it is hurting our ability as organizations to utilize what is now approximately half of the available workforce!

This inability is not simply an inconvenience, it can make or break our organization in the years ahead. Why? Well, Baby Boomers continue to recede from the workforce as they retire and Gen Z continues to enter the workforce...because kids keep growing. Strange how nature works, right?!? So, if we are struggling to find a way to connect (attract, motivate and retain) with Gen Y and Gen Z today, it is only going to get worse for us ahead. The reason we are struggling to connect is essentially because we are trying to lead them in the ways we and prior generations were led; and the values that resonated with prior generations do not resonate as loudly with Gen Y and Gen Z.

Remember Maslow's Hierarchy of Needs?

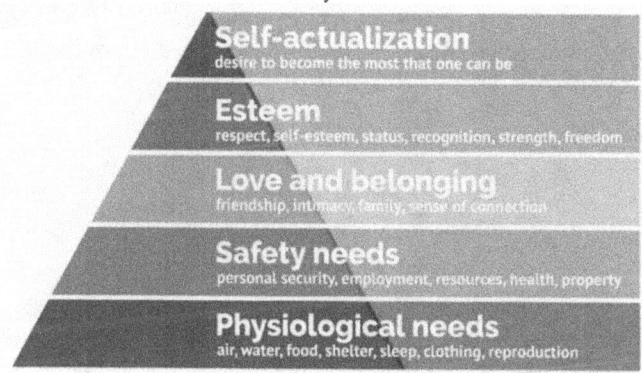

Summarily, as humans we must first ascertain lower levels of the pyramid before we may ascend upward to higher goals. If we are starving, homeless...we cannot put significant effort towards status and recognition. To climb the pyramid, I must take it one level at a time.

Why does this matter? Let me connect a few dots that are foundational pillars here. First, remember my definition of a "boss." The worst person you ever worked for in your life. Secondly, remember traditionalists and how they would do what must be done, without much complaint? Considering Traditionalists...where were they on the pyramid? They were on the bottom levels. It was survival. As traditionalists managed to find work, which was necessary in order for them to survive, do you suppose that they would put up with a "boss" and continue to keep coming back to work? Absolutely. They would put up with authoritarian, uncaring bosses who would say elitist things such as, "Your reward is your paycheck"; "Shut up and do it or go home"; "You are lucky the Company is willing to provide you an income"...and they would do it. They had to.

Remember now that I mentioned every generation is standing on the shoulders of the generations before them, and have higher expectations? We can take that concept and do a direct side-by-side of Maslow's Hierarchy with Generations to get an idea of the way Leaders must connect with our people (including Generations) to be effective at motivating them over time.

Where is the Generation?

This view is not intended to say that Gen Y and Gen Z are up in the Esteem and Self-actualization levels of the pyramid; I don't have enough evidence to say that for certain. There are certainly many anecdotal pieces of evidence that strongly suggest it though.

What I can say with a crystal-clear conscience is where Gen Y and Gen Z are not. They are not where the traditionalists were. Therefore, if you take a "boss" approach that worked for Traditionalists and tried to use it on Gen Y and Gen Z…all I can tell you is "good luck!" They have much higher expectations. If you say to them, "Your reward is your paycheck, shut up and do it or go home" …they are likely to go home and now you are left with another open slot and continuing to churn through poor retention rates in the organization. You are literally creating your own misery.

When we try to engage Gen Y & Z in this way, they end up leaving at the first break or lunch and we simply start to create those myths about them such as they are "lazy and entitled." Even worse, the "word on the street" about your company is not good and you've now hurt yourself another way: your organization is much less attractive to potentially available employees. You are creating compounding problems and a competitive disadvantage for your organization in the battlefield of available workers. If you stubbornly stick to this approach because it is the way you've always done things, then I must say for the second time, "Good luck!"

For decades work was all about money; therefore, organizations were all about money. The original "Three P's" for organizations were, "Profit, Profit, Profit!" That is what resonated with Baby Boomers and has continued to carry over…but with each generation the echo gets quieter and quieter. We are expecting more. Money for work is an expectation; therefore, getting a paycheck is a bare minimum requirement. Getting a paycheck, job titles and working endless hours of overtime is not a motivator today as it once was. We cannot lean on it as heavily as before and expect it to have the same impact on available employees.

The Three P's for Gen Y & Z are not Profit Profit Profit…so what are they? Multiple studies on Gen Y & Z show that a large percentage of them want to work for organizations that are socially and environmentally involved and an even larger percentage of them want a job with meaning beyond simply getting paid. A reasonable set of Three P's for today are: "People, Planet, Profit." Likely in that order!

Do not be discouraged if you feel confused about how your organization aligns with People and Planet…you likely already have some programs that resonate with those categories. Recycling, coats for kids, food banks…many organizations are already doing "something" and building off of that is typically low cost/no cost and low tech/no tech. The challenge question here is to simply consider if you take credit and advantage of what you already do in your efforts to attract, motivate and retain employees? Do our offer letters simply speak to income, vacation, etc., or do we also mention our social and environmental accomplishments?

The last thing I want to say in this chapter is to remember not to confuse things that are maturity related with things that are generationally related. When I hear a hiring manager say something like, "These kids are lazy and entitled" I like to immediately ask what they think the Baby Boomers said about me when I was a new worker? The same things we complain about today. Remember, some things are simply kids being kids and nothing to do with the generation.

2 CONNECTING WITH GEN Y & Z

We will break this section into three primary chunks: Attracting, Motivating and Retaining. Additionally, let me take this opportunity to translate why this matters into a language we all understand: money.

Have you ever considered, or calculated the financial impact of having to replace an employee? If you haven't, the following table is a good idea starter or template to start to sort out what it costs the organization to replace people.

A Method for Calculating Turnover Costs

Departed Employee Daily Salary + Benefits ($300.00)	Calculated Daily Cost to Cover the Position (i.e. overtime) ($150.00)
Expected Days to Fill the Position 45 days $150 x 45= $6750	Hours expected to screen resumes and interview 30 hours
HR/Hiring Managers Hourly Rate ($40.00) x 30 = $1200	Trainer Hourly Rate ($30.00)
New Hire Hourly Rate ($20.00)	Total Training Hours Planned ($20+$30) x 16 Hours= 800
Number of Working Days in first 3 Months (Productivity Ramp Up) 60 days	Total Cost to Fill Vacant Position $8750.00 – not including advertising, "new hire" quality/productivity issues...etc

As I frequently work with organizations and they

put together a cost analysis for turnover, the numbers I commonly see are between $4500 and $7000. It is a powerful realization for most of us when we run the math out because we realize not only is it frustrating to put in all the work to screen applicants, interview applicants and begin onboarding new hires…but then when we realize that new hire doesn't last we've also just poured more money into that black hole of ineffective leadership/inability to connect.

<u>Attracting Gen Y & Z to your Organization.</u>

Where are they searching for jobs? Online? Sure…but where online? Let me tell you what isn't very effective: the sign you bought at your local sign-shop that you stuck in the lawn in front of your building. Especially if it simply says, "We're hiring! Great pay! Great Benefits!" Guess what? You sound just like everyone else with a sign on their lawn, which is average; and average is not a competitive advantage.

Are there reviews of what it is like to work at your place where they are online? What are the reviews saying about your workplace?

Do they know someone who already works with your organization? If so, what is the "word on the street" about working there? Do not under-estimate what the community says about working there and how the community views the organization. Multiple sources show that Gen Z specifically prefers and relies predominantly on referrals from an employer's current and former employees! Job boards and company websites are very close together for second place. With that view in mind, what does your company website say about working there? Does it go above and beyond a link to "open positions?" Do you mention the positive social and environmental topics you are involved in as an organization?

It is reasonably obvious once we think about it, but we haven't all necessarily thought about it: these workers grew up with technology so any presence we can create through virtual platforms is more likely to reach these employees.

Do you have a presence at places they may volunteer? People, Planet, Profit. Do the organizational values match the values of the employee? Regarding environmental and safety – does the organization strive to be compliant, or strive to be world class? Keep it clean. Put people first. Take credit where credit is due and especially for work you are likely already doing that align with People Plant Profit.

Motivating Gen Y & Z in the workplace.

First things first- there are multiple motivational theories out there and conceptually many are sound. However, let's get specific here, and then we'll expand further in Chapter 5.

Keep them from getting bored. Many of our work activities can become mundane, repetitive and boring. What can we do about that? Well, remember, there are always things at work that we have to do, and then there are things at work we want to do. Don't get stuck on only what must be done; ask yourself what else the employee might be interested in at the workplace. Safety committee? Peer review board? Continuous Improvement projects? Do not fall into false limitations such as "I need a machine to run 8 hours, there's nothing I can do to make that more challenging and exciting." Completely false.

Feedback is important! No news is…bad news! Gen Y & Z want frequent feedback. This one is exceptionally odd for many of us older generations. We tended to view this exactly the opposite: no news is good news! This meant that if we didn't hear from the "boss" that meant we weren't doing anything wrong. It also is a strong indicator of management by exception when we live in that "no news is good news world"; which can unintentionally create a toxic environment in which perception becomes "no one says anything about the 99 things I did right, all I hear about is that one thing…"

Remembering again that these workers grew up with technology, consider the ways you may give frequent feedback through digital tools & platforms. Rewards and recognition via a company Facebook or Twitter page? On your internal CCTV's?

Following that point: focus on positives. Don't use "accountability" only when something goes wrong. That type of accountability only fosters blame and resentment. Negative accountability usually creeps in through side conversations within small groups who blame everyone else for everything that goes wrong. Think of the rumor mill. I won't ask if your organization struggles with a rumor mill; I already know the answer for most of you. Don't let that become the main or loudest narrative. A significant part of feedback should be praise related, and not held back for special "herculean" accomplishments. Catch people doing the right things. Create those positive "high-five" moments and watch the enthusiasm spread. This is not conceptual, I've lived it; it works.

Another motivational pro-tip: provide structure via mentoring and great training. This may seem obvious; my only "yeah but" here is then why do I continuously see organizations under-respect training? Unfortunately, many organizations still view a training program as something along the lines of, "Fill out these forms and acknowledgements, watch this safety video we bought in 1989, and follow that person over there for six weeks." As mentioned earlier in regards to entitlement, this type of onboarding approach is obviously, blatantly not world class and is being more commonly rejected by employees who have higher expectations for the organizations they choose to work for. This particular topic is another direct insight into what it is like at a workplace; and is frequently discussed in reviews and referrals between potential employees as they consider your organization. "World on the street" for places that train like this starts to sound like, "Oh they just throw you to the wolves there, they don't train you on anything and then they yell at you for making mistakes." Doesn't sound very appealing to potential new hires, does it? Your organization will start steadily moving down the list of preferred jobs in the area to have. Good luck.

Gen Y and Z have a very strong desire to keep learning. Your organization will have a competitive advantage if you have continuing education opportunities to go along with the frequent feedback and interaction with mentors and leaders. When I say continuing education I don't mean "give tuition reimbursement." What I mean is be considerate of their future pathways for growth and utilize your understanding of where they aspire to be in the future to take advantage of continuous learning opportunities. To clarify here, just like I would have done with other leaders I would grow (independent of Generation), I would be lining up a Performance Management Plan to stretch & grow the individual in line with future Org Chart needs and plans. Know your people. Look ahead. Make specific plans. Be a professional with development and continuous learning; you won't regret it.

Part of what I just mentioned means you have to know your people. As a leader, there is no excuse for you not to know them anyway. If you don't, you are assuredly already being viewed as a "boss" right now.

Motivation is, has always been, and shall always be a moving target; independent of generation or job title or salary. As a leader, you have to know your people to start to understand what get's them truly connected to Vision, Mission and Values.

Retaining Gen Y & Z in the workplace.

Relationships matter. Gen Y & Z are not loyal to brands; they will not take the company flag home and plant it on their front lawn. Being a massive organization is a lot less appealing to these folks; in fact, it can be a disadvantage because they know people in large organizations tend to be more systems driven, bureaucratic and blindly follow processes even when they go against logic. There tends to be that lack of willingness or ability to do what is right in one-off situations and they tend to have too many "stupid and archaic rules."

Kill stupid archaic rules. Imagine if you will what may have been said by the "old timers" as vehicles were becoming widely available and used last century. "These kids today are too lazy to saddle a horse, and too impatient to ride one! I think they should do it the way I've always done it! Therefore, we shall only have horse and buggy parking available for our employees. If they want to drive a car they can work somewhere else!"

What might be viewed as stupid rules? Dress code? Cell phones not allowed in the workplace? Staying until 5pm even when all the work is done? Let's get a little more uncomfortable…what about attendance point systems? This one particularly rubs a lot of Leaders the wrong way because it is so uncomfortable to consider letting go of a mechanism many of us have used for decades to try and drive attendance. I can't yet say it is something to do; but it is something to consider. I have two clients whom have abandoned their "point systems" and simply said to their employees, "We trust you will come to work when you can." So far, attendance has actually gone up at these places! Very counter-intuitive for "bosses" who think we have to make people do what we want, but it makes sense for leaders whom understand trust and positive reinforcement typically get greater results. To be transparent though, this is still a highly untested approach. Two clients are not a large sample size…but the point is, be willing to scrutinize what you have always done. If you do what you've always done, you'll get what you always got. Maybe don't force them to occupy a chair because some clock on the wall says it is the time for that chair to be filled and we've always stayed until 5:00pm.

Do you and your organization currently have "stupid, archaic rules?" Well, here are two great questions to ask yourself in pursuit of that answer.

1. Do we have a rule that we do not consistently enforce (or just don't enforce at all)? If that answer is yes (and really be honest on these questions, out of respect for yourself and your organization), then you are probably creating an environment that, at best, teaches employees that it is ok to break rules; and at worst if being unevenly enforced you are creating a perception in the employees that there is favoritism because some employees have a rule enforced while others do not.
2. Do we have rules that create barriers to hiring and retaining available workers? I don't care what a company offered me as a salary, if I have to drive a horse and buggy to park there, I'm not working there!

Celebrate success. Here's an easy one: when you have an employee complete a real training program, do we even congratulate them? Think of it this way- you likely remember your work anniversary date; the date you were hired. Have you ever worked somewhere for three, four, or more years…and on your anniversary date not one single person says anything about it? How does that make you feel? It is a disconnector. New hires who make it through training are typically proud of that achievement; and often times it goes unnoticed or unspoken. Why not print a certificate of completion with the company branding on it? Why not put it on the CCTV's in the building? Celebration is easy, remembering to do it is the hard bit.

Communication and Teamwork. Right words, right time. Collaborate to win together. Let's emphasize this one for a moment by connecting a few previous points together. If I understand feedback is important, and collaboration is important, and mentoring and training…while also remembering they are digitally inclined and confident…then I absolutely should allow them to share their ideas and talents (such as digital knowledge) with older workers. This is a double bonus activity; not only does it create engagement and show appreciation to what Gen Y & Z bring to the table right away, it also helps them and those older workers start to create peer connections which is a massively important step in overall employee retention! Collaborate to win together; start it early and do it often. It will do amazing things for culture and for preventing future conflicts in the workplace, especially between generations and generational styles.

Many organizations already struggle with communication; this can get worse if we try to force our employees to communicate in ways we like rather than in ways they prefer. Don't blame a communication gap on, or as, a generational gap. There are an abundance of communication options above and beyond old fashioned email…or even older fashioned pen & paper. I personally have seen many organizations utilizing Google Hangouts for across shift communication, for example. We should understand that those types of communications platforms are only going to become more the "norm" and less the "exception." Don't make the mistake I made years ago. I remember when text messages were new and I thought to myself, "This fad is never going to last. I have Nextel push-to-talk, which takes two seconds. Why would I spend three minutes typing a message when I can simply say it so much faster?" I admit now, I was wrong on that. The way we prefer to communicate has always changed and that will only continue.

Let's follow that up just a little because communication is so very critical in every organization. Does your organization tend to speak in slightly archaic codes? What I mean is, are you a fan of formal communication styles? If so, it may be something to consider getting uncomfortable with. Gen Z specifically is losing/has already lost a lot of barriers between work, personal and social life. They're not really very separate anymore; it may actually be impossible to say "work life" and "home life" and "social life" as separate entities. More and more, there is just "life" and they're all blended together. The point? Casual, informal communication is becoming (and will continue to become) the norm, not the exception. Prudish, formal communicators are going to be viewed likely in a negative, archaic way.

Additionally, what is "face to face" communication no longer means what many of us prior generations consider face to face. With Gen Z, almost everything that can be done physically can also be done digitally. Think about going to Walmart. I get in my car, drive over and buy groceries. It feels awkward for me to order it online…but I certainly can. To that point, it does not feel awkward for Gen Z. If they drive to Walmart and put stuff in a cart, it is exactly the same to them to simply go to the website and put stuff in the digital cart. Zero difference. This carries over to communication. Face to face, for many Gen Z, includes Facetiming, Zoom, and Google Hangouts. Those variations are just the same to them as sitting in a conference room at a table together.

As a Leader, I can be uncomfortable but willing to communicate in ways that actually reach my audience, or I can be uncomfortable with the results of poor communication because I do it my way. Choose wisely.

One final note for this section: do you, as the reader, remember what it was like to start working for a company and spend your entire career at that one single company? If so, I'm pretty sure I can guess which generation you are from.

When did the expectation start to die off that we, as individuals, would go to work at a company and stay there for life? **Decades ago.** **<u>Multiple decades ago!</u>**

Why did that expectation start to die off? Well, let's be honest. American companies started not keeping people for their entire careers. That expectation was killed primarily by the organizations now complaining no one "sticks around" for life. It is rather ironic to me that a few generations ago, workers were mainly willing to be "lifers" until that option was taken off the table by organizations themselves.

What's the point of this note? We, as prior generations, have created current generations whom are absolutely comfortable with "gig" work…out of necessity. There are virtually zero expectations from Gen Y & Gen Z to spend an entire career at once place. That mere concept sounds ridiculous, inconceivable, absurd. Furthermore, for several years now most of us view having an employee with a length of service of 4 to 5 years as successful. This comfort level with "gig" work is critical to understand as leaders because it is simply another reason why the classic "boss" approach has become poisonous to our employee retention efforts. Gen Y & Z essentially has no fear about losing a job; whether it is their decision or not…it is already an expectation. The job they have now, will be lost. It's part of life; it is the norm.

Remember that, before you "threaten" an employee with termination. That threat has essentially no value. Additionally, it is more likely the employee will just go ahead and leave right then, or within a day or two based on that "boss-like" threat. Some people like to toss that threat around like candy. Again, "Good luck!"

Last thing to add here- watch out for burnout. For the skeptical reader with pre-conceived notions, bias and assumptions about these generations this may be difficult to believe, but it is a real concern. These generations are very competitive, and when properly engaged, extremely hard working. I've seen them, and continue to see them all the time as I travel and work with various organizational. Just because your organization may be struggling with them, believe me, others are thriving with them. Back to the point here- watch for burn out. Especially since the Covid-19 driven "work from home" reality for many positions, Gen Y & Z especially have been hit hard regarding mental health, depression, anxiety and burnout. If you are starting to connect some foundational dots, this will make perfect sense to you. If not, let me help move the logic along.

If I understand that Gen Y & Z are heavily "connected" to the internet, et al their entire (or most) of their lives, and I understand that, to them, there really isn't much difference between a Teams or WebEx meeting than meeting in real life, then here is what that means: they really struggle with **disconnecting**. So, if work is now something they do remotely, and they don't really understand disconnecting, they really struggle to understand when their day starts and stops. Therefore, for many of them, it doesn't stop! I have the luxury of being Gen X and spending a large portion of my life with no internet; therefore, for me disconnecting is easy. With a motivated, driven Gen Y & Z employee, it may feel unnatural to disconnect. If they don't disconnect, they kind of never "leave work." Imagine what that must feel like, never leaving work. We do ourselves a service (and them) when he occasionally "orient to the obvious"; i.e. perhaps simply saying, crystal clear, "Hey, make sure you stop checking emails after 5:00pm. You must have some time in which work is not where your mind is."

A large helper to retaining your workforce whom work remotely would be to keep this consideration in mind: help them understand that each day should have an ending, and disconnecting is naturally and necessary! Also don't be shy about your EAP's (Employee Assistance Programs) that is already part of your insurance; they can reach out and talk to someone as they feel these mental health and burnout issues. It's already covered by your insurance.

3 YOUR TEAM'S PERFORMANCE IS A DIRECT REFLECTION OF YOUR PERFORMANCE AS A LEADER

This goes right back to the title- The Field Does Not Come to the Farmer. What does that mean? It means to be a successful Leader I have to engage, empower and motivate my Team. In order to achieve this, I have to meet people where they are, not where I want them to be. A farmer cannot farm from his porch; and a Leader cannot lead by shouting from an ivory tower. For the farmer to be successful, he must go to the field and cultivate. It is the same with us as Leaders.

We judge Leaders the same way we judge coaches: as measured by their Team's success. Individual success rolls up to Team success; Team success rolls up to departmental success; departmental success rolls up to organizational success.

Our Teams shall always be diverse. This includes age, values, beliefs, abilities, disabilities, communication styles…etc. You will not have the luxury of only hiring people who like to communicate the same way you do, following up the previous example recently given. If I understand this, then I must understand the burden of reaching people's hearts and minds is on me as a Leader. I must flex to them in the place that gets them going rather than using my preferred style and trying to bend the world to my way. It doesn't work, and it only wears you out while creating disconnects with our people.

Additionally, Gen Y & Z are coming into workplaces where diversity and inclusion are the norm; at the forefront. They take it extremely seriously; not simply checking a box. They want to drive a more diverse and inclusive workplace, which includes the way we communicate, and being genuine about communication and the style we use.

With that in mind, consider Dr. Paul Hersey's "The Situational Leader." Summarily it states that leaders will have four types of employees (followers and their readiness level; R1, R2, R3, R4) and as a leader we must be competent in matching the appropriate leadership style (S1, S2, S3, S4) to get the most out of our people. R1 type followers need to be told what to do and watched fairly closely; think of your new hires or struggling employees for this category. They need an S1 leadership style; we have to tell them what to do. These folks benefit from our management systems while they grow.

R2 type followers and R3 type followers are more competent but perhaps confused or disconnected for various reasons to some degree. The goal is to move these people in the right direction and get the most from them that I possibly can as a Leader. Therefore, they take an S2 and S3 leadership style. S2 summarily means connecting them with "why" we do things the way we do them; it is an important connection to make. S3 summarily means we get their participation in the way we do things; they have a voice and are respected as subject matter experts in the work they do. My favorite way to explain that style is the formula $R = Q \times A$. My ***results*** as a leader depend on the ***quality*** of my procedures times the ***acceptance*** of my people to follow those procedures. If I asked you, "do you have job procedures or work instructions at your organization?" many of us say yes, we do. If I then ask you, "Do your people always follow your procedures?" many of us say, "Sometimes." To me, sometimes means no they do not.

Here is a pro-tip; there are two primary reasons people do not follow our job procedures in our organization (independent of industry). The first is that we do not explain "why" our procedures are the way they are. This is really simple, but most of us haven't thought about it. Our procedures are "the best way we know today to do this task." Explain that to people because they want to know why.

The second reason is that many organizations develop their procedures from a high-level view. I take my process engineer and I have them utilize a flow chart and observation techniques to figure out the best way to perform a task. Then we write that up into a procedure and deliver it to the frontline workers and tell them, "This is the best way to do your job." There is a major flaw in that approach. Consider this: who knows how to do their job better than the process engineer or the supervisor? The people who do it all day long every day of the week. If I understand that, then why don't I ask them to help us as an organization figure out the real best way to do their job? My view is that we, as leaders, should set the wide boundaries to ensure employee ideas do not break safety or quality…and then give them a loud voice in how we "do the doing."

When I take that approach, I typically get higher quality processes (and they match the way it actually is done in real life, rather than the paper not matching the actual process). Along with that, and more importantly, I get the acceptance of my people to follow those procedures because we support what we create! Therefore, my results as a leader climb higher because my Team's performance climbs higher. $R = Q \times A$.

To drill that out further, I emphasize that as leaders we spend a disproportionate amount of time and effort on categories that don't have much return on the investment. As a leader, consider how much of your time is spent on "problem" employees, or your R1's that you have to manage and "tell them what to do." Historically for many of us, it is a significant amount of time; especially if we manage by exception focusing only on the things that can go wrong. Realize this though, R1 type employees typically make up a small percentage of your Teams. If, for simple math, they represent 10% of our Team (and that is likely an exaggerated percentage, typically it is less than that), then why do we tend to give them 80% of our focus. 80% of our horsepower. 80% of our time.

They, at best, represent a 10% return on the investment I give them. If I want bang for my buck, because I am not an infinite resource and I value my time, then I have to consciously ensure I do not get "stuck" giving disproportionate effort and time to what is truly a small opportunity and, by the way, is the type of folks whom which we have management systems for anyway! This is where you lean on your management system to work for you instead of against you. This is why we create those systems!

Let your management systems resolve your R1 employees to free you up and focus on your R2's and R3's because they typically represent 80% of your employees; therefore, they represent your biggest opportunity to influence people with your Leadership. Additionally, we must remember that if I do not lead with intent, then I am subjected to the randomness of people doing what they do as they feel like it…and my R2's and R3's are commonly shifting somewhat towards becoming R4's or R1's. Do I want my negligence as a leader to create more R1's? Absolutely not. Again, emphasis is on Leading with Intent!

So, summarily, as Leaders we should devote 80% of

our time connecting our Team with "why" we do things the way we do and allowing them to help us continuously improve the way we do things through R = Q x A.

To not forget the last follower readiness category: R4's are our people who aspire to grow, to be challenged, who want "more." To lead them, using the S4 style…give it to them. Delegate. They want it, and it builds a deeper wider foundation for the Team. Everyone wins when we engage our R4 employee types.

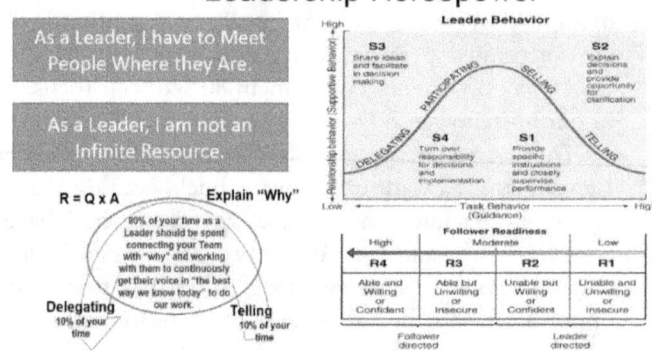

4 LEADERSHIP BEHAVIOR DICTATES CULTURE

Culture eats technical skills all day every day. What I mean by that is a team of experts is only as successful as their ambitions and goals. High I.Q. does not necessarily mean high performance! Even experts among experts are not very effective if they aren't motivated or, even worse, disconnected because of a poor leadership style. An organization like this will never reach its full sense of entitlement. Related to Gen Y & Z, having a great culture is a significant way of bridging generational gaps between Boomers, Gen X, Gen Y and Gen Z. Shared experiences and culture give commonality among differing generations; which helps build trust and relationships.

Culture building, believe it or not, is a process. With that in mind, it should be treated as something to do with intent (just like Leadership). Your organization will have a culture one way or another; and if you aren't driving the culture then you are at the mercy of getting whatever you get and it may not be the culture you wish you had.

The natural question with that understanding in mind is, "How do I create and drive a culture?"

The best answer is also the simplest answer: by Leadership actions. Our leaders are where our employees feel trusted…or not. Where they feel respected…or not. Valued…or not. I don't care what your policies, procedures, mission vision values are; all the things we write on paper mean nothing compared with the daily operating norms. Think of it this way: imagine we start our work day off with a meeting. We believe in safety, so every meeting starts with a safety share, right? Then after the meeting we all go out to the workplace and on our way out people see me step around a spilled a mop bucket. It wasn't me who spilled it, so I simply walk on by it. My actions just communicated loud and clear how I really feel about safety. Then the word in the organization becomes that we don't actually care about safety, we just talk about safety. That spills over into the culture, which spills into the daily operating norms.

As leaders we must understand that we cast a larger shadow than we may realize. We are setting examples all the time, even when we do not intend to.

How does this relate to Gen Y and Gen Z? Because they tend to not only respond to action like generations before them, but they tend to take action. Part of their desire to have meaning beyond a paycheck means not sitting on the sidelines complaining, but getting on the field and doing something! If you've ever had someone say to you, "That's not my job" in the workplace and it rubbed you the wrong way…let me tell you that you are far less likely to hear that from Gen Y & Z. There is actually some reason for optimism that Gen Y & Z will be better leaders than generations before them because they don't just "talk about it"; they want to "be about it." That is beautiful and powerful.

Also understand this- everything is instantaneous these days. Except job satisfaction and strength of relationships (not to be confused with number of relationships). The things that really matter usually take time, which means they take patience. The concern is that folks do not stay at the workplace long enough for this process to take the time it requires to take to build a great culture. Tactical trick? Start right now building it with intent. Let it begin to grow and then capture and cascade it into everything you do including your new hire training. Start speaking and leading from a cultural view minute one day one with your new hires. Don't over focus on short term gains; caring more about the metrics than the person. This is where directly an organization's poor leadership can create a toxic culture…or not. Leadership is, again, about people, not processes.

Focus on purpose (why, and $R = Q \times A$) first and metrics second. The metrics will get in line when you focus on purpose but when we focus on metrics first the purpose gets lost and the metrics suffer. We don't reach our full sense of entitlement. It is more important to get things right than to get them fast.

This is where I will introduce the House of Leadership. The House of Leadership represents the pillars and building blocks of culture development.

Leader Behavior & Culture		
Engagement	*Respect*	*Transparency*
Utilize Employees KSA	Listen Actively	Communicate Often
Catch People Doing the "Right" Things	Provide Autonomy where possible	Admit Mistakes
Discover & Develop Plans to meet Employee Goals	Show "Thank You"	Lead with "Why"

Attract
Motivate
Retain

The house of Leadership is something I developed to visually show the way Leaders directly influence Culture. I have to emphasize again that Culture should be viewed as a process and developed actively; or your organization's culture will be determined by the loudest people in the company who talk the most.

This was not put together specifically in mind for Gen

Y and Gen Z but translates extremely well to them. This is no surprise because, as I've mentioned in various ways, they are really no different than other generations except for their expectations and values. People are people are people. I don't care what generation, what job title, what salary…we are all people.

The engagement pillar is one to emphasize because I hear many organizations say they want their people to be "engaged and empowered" but what does that mean? That is where many of us struggle. We don't know what it looks like, feels like, smells like…therefore, we don't know how to achieve it. Engagement, in my very concise description, can be described in three words: Connection, Purpose, Ownership.

If you look at my House of Leadership, you'll notice all the building blocks under the Engagement and Respect Pillars speak to that "engagement and empowerment" we all want to achieve.

The third pillar is pointed more inwardly towards the leader, emphasizing authenticity and being a credible human being, which builds trust with our Teams. When it comes to Leadership, by the way, *personal credibility is more important to our followers than personal competency*. That's because what we do is about the Team, not about ourselves. Again, when our Team's are successful, only then are we successful as Leaders. Focus on Team success, the rest takes care of itself.

Let's briefly step through the 3 building blocks under the Engagement Pillar.
1. Utilize Employees' Knowledge, Skills & Abilities.
    a. R=QxA
    b. With Gen Y & Z, where possible, embrace (or at least enable) them to utilize the tools and technology they are comfortable with. It can help retention today; and honestly those tools and

technologies are likely to be the norm in five years anyway.
2. Catch People doing the "Right Things."
   a. Focus on positive reinforcement. Pride matters more than money for many incumbent workers.
3. Discover & Develop plans to meet Employee Goals.
   a. First, you should know your people. Second, know who aspires to be "more" in the organization than they currently are.
   b. This is not just focused on org chart progression; not everyone wants org chart progression. This is about connecting with individuals where they are within what they have interests in.

Next, let's step through the Respect Pillar.
1. Listen Actively.
   a. Listen with the intent to hear; not with the intent to reply.
   b. Listening is easy when it is easy. The pros are able to listen completely, even when they strongly disagree with what they are hearing.
2. Provide Autonomy Where Possible.
   a. Create an atmosphere in which you, as a Leader, could randomly disappear for an entire day, unannounced, and the Team has no idea. The Team should not need the coach on the field to play successfully.
3. Show Thank You.
   a. Of course, say thank you…but remember that our actions speak louder than our words? Show Thank you.

Lastly, the Transparency Pillar.
1. Communicate Often.

    a. It is better to over communicate than under communicate; and honestly it is very difficult to actually over communicate. How will people see my vision if I cannot find a way to put it in the mind of the receiver (my employee)?
2. Admit Mistakes.
    a. Do NOT fake it until you make it. Your people do not expect you to be perfect, they do expect you to be consistent. If you are unwilling to admit mistakes, you actually under-cut your own credibility as a Leader. No one is perfect, not even you.
    b. Specific to Gen Y & Z, especially Gen Z, they value authenticity above all else in leaders.
3. Lead with "Why."
    a. The way most of us are wired, we always want to know "why". When toddlers learn to speak, they use the word "why" a lot for a reason!
    b. Guess what, we don't outgrow that desire to know why. We may sometimes teach ourselves to stop asking why, but it doesn't make us stop wondering why.

5 TOTAL REWARDS WITH AN EMPHASIS ON INTRINSIC AND EXTRINSIC VALUES FOR GEN Y & Z

Total Rewards is one of the Six Disciplines within Human Resource Management. It focuses on the development and implementation of compensation and benefit programs that attract, motivate and retain employees. Total Rewards is comprised of two main scopes: Monetary and Non-Monetary. We will focus on the non-monetary side for several reasons but most importantly because people will start working with you for money, but that is not what will keep them working with you.

On the non-monetary view, we will drill that out into two types of rewards: Intrinsic and Extrinsic. Intrinsic Rewards are the things that a person values, feels satisfaction and a sense of pride simply from doing. They need no external input to achieve this feeling. Extrinsic rewards are those feelings as they are achieved from others via praise, recognition and the like.

Relative to Gen Y & Gen Z, here are some examples of each in the following table.

Intrinsic	Extrinsic
Growth	The relationship with their supervisor
Exciting Work	Visibility, Empowerment
Challenging Work	Performance Feedback
Self-Direction	Industry Certification
Praising & Recognizing Others	Working with people they like
Being Innovative	Having a voice as part of a Team
Feeling Inspired	Bonuses
Being a Subject Matter Expert	Being Utilized as a Subject Matter Expert
Leaving things better than they found them	Merit Based Reviews
Volunteering	Given more responsibilities
Winning Competitions	Plaques, Certificates
Not being micromanaged	Structure

We can take this view and link it with McClelland's Acquired Needs theory to get a beautiful summation of how, no matter how much things change over time regarding values, we are all people at the end of the day. McClelland's theory states essentially that emotional satisfaction may be achieved through a combination of Achievement (getting things done); Power (having influence over others); and Affiliation (having good relationships). We simply should recognize that Gen Y and Gen Z have the same emotional drivers as other generations; it is simply the mechanics of what those drivers are that are different. Every person, independent of generation, has an invisible sign around their neck that says, "Make me feel important." Fundamentally, connect with them in the way that gets their gears going.

McClelland's Acquired Needs

- Achievement (getting things done)
- Power (having influence over others)
- Affiliation (having good relationships)

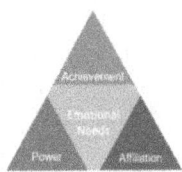

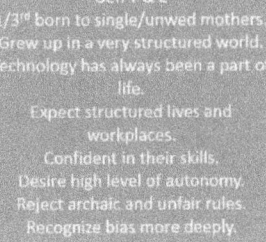

Gen Y & Z
1/3rd born to single/unwed mothers.
Grew up in a very structured world.
Technology has always been a part of life.
Expect structured lives and workplaces.
Confident in their skills.
Desire high level of autonomy.
Reject archaic and unfair rules.
Recognize bias more deeply.

Learn to ask ourselves questions like, "Is this the best we can do regarding recycling?" "Do we have alternative chemicals that have less impact on the people and the environment?" Do we have a social club option where people whom are so inclined can step up and help with Red Cross blood donations, food bank drives, etc.?" These types of things can quickly turn into low cost/no cost and low tech/no tech options that Gen Y and Gen Z may connect to in order to help them achieve their emotional satisfaction by creating opportunities to get more than "a paycheck" while being employed at your organization.

Where to start? Well if we look at some generalities of what was/is shaping Gen Y & Z from their formative years, then we can begin to directly translate that into our own specific organizational outreach opportunities. In the figure above are just a few notes about Gen Y & Z regarding their formative years; but let's unpack them a little to get your ideas flowing.

- 1/3rd born to single/unwed mothers.

Relevance? They witnessed the ability of a lone individual to be successfully self reliant. Therefore, they understand that they don't "need" anyone else. Depend on no one except yourself and you'll be fine. This is a large reason they are so confident; they've seen how powerful one person can be at accomplishing the important things in life (even if it wasn't easy).

- Grew up in a very structured world.

Relevance? There is an expectation that people do what they have agreed to do and planning is critical to success. Getting surprised with a failure of that is a tremendous, potentially deal breaking failure. Consider- daycare, school, after school activities. They get shuffled to daycare before school. Then they go to school from daycare; then they return to daycare after school. Then a parent picks them up and gets dinner done, goes over homework, etc. Think about all the moving parts involved in that typical day and all the interrelated people involved in that process…simply for a child to be taken care for one single day. That is a lot of planning and teamwork. Prior generations, perhaps "Mom" stayed at home and did all of these things (especially for Baby Boomers). It was a lot less complicated, and also less structured in that view than the view for what Gen Y & Gen Z have experienced. So if they are used to seeing a very structured life and then they come to work for you and you "throw them to the wolves" in your training program due to a lack of structure and planning, it is immediately disconnecting and disconcerting.

- Technology has always been a part of their life.

Relevance? I recall when cell phones were new (and rare & expensive). I recall when the internet was new and we were all discovering what the "world wide web" was. Many of Gen Y & Z have absolutely no concept of that world. For them, it never existed. For myself, I liken it to me never having lived in a world without radio or television. How unnatural would it feel for me to suddenly not have access to a television or radio? We must have some understanding when we notice how important cell phones are, for example, to Gen Y & Z. I can assure you that technology is not going away, it is only going to increase in frequency, use and variety.

- Expect Structured Lives and Workplaces.

Relevance? Imagine your new hire shows up for their first

day, and their laptop isn't ready, or their email isn't set up, or you have them sitting around for 45 minutes while you find the right people to start their training or you tell them to go "shadow someone" for today and it all seems very random (and likely is). How can we realistically expect them to see an entire organization with all of their resources have such a haphazard and unstructured approach to orientation and not be judgemental? Why? Well, they saw their single mother working full time and also maybe taking classes part time and she was able to set up such a structured world for them with the daycare and the sports and the after school activities…and she was able to do that, again, as one person. Now they are seeing 10, 100, or more people whom can't even manage to have a smooth continous flow of introducing a new hire into the workforce properly? Sorry folks, but I agree. That is unacceptable. They recognize that as a clear indicator that the organization is not world class; not even close. They also understand that means, in their daily worklives there, most things will probably be "by the seat of their pants" and reactive; panic and emergency situations frequently. Additionally, it is an indicator that they will likely be treated as a number, not a name. No thanks.

- Confident in their skills.

Relevance? Will absolutely challenge the "way we've always done things." Also ready to be Plant Manager in three weeks after starting…just ask them! To me, this is a great problem to have with employees. As a leader I need to harness that enthusiasm into a structured development plan and let the benefits start to accrue for the employee and the organization. This is something to take advantage of; not to view as an annoyance.

- Desire a high level of autonomy.

Relevance? This is why they flinch and retreat when people tell them all the "don't" things to do when training. Many things to them seem abundantly obvious; and when you say "Look out for this" and "don't do this" their mind starts to go idle with boredom. They want to focus on how to do things better and are more willing to "fail forward" than prior generations. This is great, in my opinion, because it shows that generationally perhaps we are becoming less afraid of the "fear of failure." The fear of failure is an immature, childish fear that tends to hold us back from even trying. When that happens, we do get stuck in the "way we've always done things" and do not improve. Also remember: $R = Q \times A$ is powerful for all generations, including these.

- Reject archaic and unfair rules.

Relevance? If you do what you've done, you'll get what you always got. Let's be honest, over time many organizations have developed such a bureaucratic control and command approach that we've really created impossible pathways to success and sensibility. My favorite example: the GM Dress Code Policy. It was at one (very recent!) time a full 10 pages! Consider that for a moment. Ten pages. For a dress code policy. I wish I were joking. Then Mary Barra changed it to something sensible. She took it from 10 (!) pages to two words: Dress Appropriately. Here's another pro-tip: the more words we use, the more we tie ourselves down. Don't let your schooling get in the way of your education (Mark Twain).

- Recognize Bias More Deeply

Relevance? Consider the Central Tendency Error. This is a review system that is fundamentally flawed, yet an astonishing number of organizations use it to give their employees reviews. This review system works like this:

- You have a scale of 1 to 5 to rank employees on against categories (attendance, quality, teamwork…).
- If you meet all the expectations for the category, you get a score of 3 on the scale of 5. We tell people that means that if you get a 3…that is a great score! Well done!
- We also say, "to get a 4 is nearly impossible…you

have to wildly exceed expectations. To get a 5 is impossible because that means you have no room for improvement; a 5 is absolute perfection and no one is perfect."

Let's unpack some of the flaws with this system.

First- when we set goals that are impossible to achieve, is it a motivator or a de-motivator? It is a de-motivator; and worse yet, it can become a demoralizer! In this system, someone who has perfect attendance receives a score of 3/5. Never late, never missed a day of planned work. Perfect attendance. The word perfect means perfect, right!? How does that not score as a 5? It is illogical, but because of the scale and set up of that system it is a 3. When our employees push back and ask us the obvious question, "How can I get a 4 or a 5 if I already have perfect attendance?" we tend to tell them some generic answer (because we don't know either, because the system makes no sense!). We'll say something like, "well you have to work overtime to raise that above a 3." I could possibly agree with a generic answer like that if, and only if, I have a specific criteria established. If I cannot say explicitly how many hours turns the 3 into a 4; and how many hours turns it into a 5, then it is just more nonsense trying to come up with excuses for a broken and flawed system.

Here's how it can become toxic and have the opposite effect we should be getting from a review system: take the employee above, with perfect attendance. Even if they ultimately sign the review form and stop arguing with us over the stupidity of the score not being perfect, it does not mean they now believe it. They typically have simply realized that they are being subjected to something they cannot change and therefore must accept the illogical score. They may have noticed, however, that our scale may have allowed for one or two missed days of work still being considered a score of 3...so the way our mind works is that it looks for ways to manipulate stupid systems because we don't willingly embrace stupid systems. So this perfect attendance person thinks, "Well, if I cannot control raising my score above a 3, what can I control? Hmmm…according to the scale, I can miss a few days of work in a year and it doesn't hurt."

I have personally seen employees go from a perfect annual attendance to calling in sick within a week of their review in systems like this. What an abysmal failure when a system encourages someone to regress to the norm; which leads me to the second major flaw.

Second- we should treat special people special. In this system, what we unintentionally do is take high performing people (all stars) and pull them down to average 3/5. We should be trying to raise the average, not creating a culture of average! Early in my career I was told that we have to treat people the same. That is terrible advice and fortunately I learned to throw that advice straight in the trash where it belongs.

What we have to do is to treat people fairly and in order to treat people fairly I literally cannot treat them all the same! I have absolutely no problem creating lighthouse examples out of my high-performing employees. I do not even try to sneak it in the back door or keep it a secret; I do and always shall treat special people special. In order to do this I have to be explicitly clear on what is average, what is below average and what is special; but once the criteria is clear then I put that system to work for me. It has served me well over the years taking that approach and encouraging people to strive to reach higher expectations than to settle for average. When I've heard the occasional person saying something along the lines of, "you are playing favorites" I have no shame in (politely and professionally) telling them that I do not; because my criteria is crystal clear. I also follow that up every time by saying, "If you want to be treated special, then get special." I am rooting for every employee to be the best they want to be.

I do want to be clear here on another important

part of this view: I don't expect every employee to be high performers and I have no issue with employees whom simply want to show up, do a good job, and go home. For my folks whom consistently do a good job and they are satisfied with simply being good, not necessarily great, that is also excellent. I'll take 100 of those types of employees all day every day. We can do amazing things with consistently good employees; I want to treat my good employees well. However, I won't treat good like it is great or I inadvertently take above average and turn it into average.

Linking this all back to biases and Gen Y & Z: a review system like this is something many prior generations recognized as wrong and biased but learned to accept. Gen Y & Z, with their higher expectations and deeper perspective of bias, are actively rejecting them. They recognize it is flawed and will not accept it. If you are competing with other organizations for available workers, and you utilize the Central Tendency Error system of reviews, you are at a competitive disadvantage for that bulk of the available workforce out there. As I like to say, if you intend to stick with an approach such as that (because you've always done it that way)...good luck!

This one example is only one of many that exist in the workplace. Do yourself a favor and start to look for them...they are certainly there in abundance and they will hurt your ability to attract, motivate and retain employees.

One further example of bias that is hard to recognize but pure insidious poison: Beware the "injector" employee. The injector employee is an employee who has earned some level of respect and recognition in the organization; they are typically recognized and rewarded due to effort and passion as well as being "homegrown". Once you learn to see one, you see them all...and they are pervasive in organizations. The injector, having gained some level of promotion, is now doing things they are not sure how to link to organizational success (because most of us get promoted to our highest level of incompetence; i.e. the "Peter Principle"). When an employee really wants to help, and really wants to do well, but is not sure how they can do that in the position they occupy...here's what they tend to do:

First, they work a lot of hours, unnecessarily. Their schedule is 8am to 5pm; but they show up at 5:30am. They stay until 5:30pm. They are always "busy" and have no time (and they like to think they have no time because they must overcome the ineptitude of other departments and their own employees). This is not usually true (and is a red flag), but in their mind, it is a satisfying answer for justifying the hours and their intrinsic value. It is also easier than looking inward on themselves and addressing their real issue: feeling a little lost, unsure and uncertain. Also, usually, they share this view with people close to them, bad-mouthing others as being inept. Again, makes them feel better (temporarily) by blaming others as sloppy, inept, not caring...whatever words they use, what they really mean is "not like me in my heroic brilliance, attitude and efforts." This is where a lot of "politics" start in the workplace.

Additionally, they tend to fall in love with "tools." This is a massive indicator. The newest software designed to do xyz; the newest database option that promises to track and trend this and that; the most powerful tools from their previous job (whether they fit the current organization or not); etc. Big red flag. They tend to fall in love with tools because of their lack of confidence combined with their internal desire to succeed. Their hope is they'll find some tool that will be their chalice or Holy Grail to suddenly leap ahead and be special again. You'll recognize this because they are always using and recommend the next greatest shiniest tool they found; which by the way also creates a lot more work for them as they continuously have to migrate information from the recent tool (or method) to the new tool (or method), leading to longer days. Lots of activity, but not a lot of productivity. Lots of passion, but usually frustration and negativity.

Then, they start getting involved in things outside of their role & responsibility. They start to jump into other people's sandbox and start moving sand around. During management meetings, they'll start to speak up and out of turn, pushing their thoughts and usually saying how their "tool" of the moment could solve all these problems everyone else is suffering. They also tend to believe it; because it has the emotional attachment of self-validation. Therefore, they can be very convincing. If an organization starts to listen and follow these people, we tend to start losing culture. Why?

This is one of the places politics and over-management begin. A minor problem comes up, and they believe you should apply the most powerful world's greatest tool on every tiny little issue and we should start forcing "standardization of tools" across the organization (which, of course is standardized against the tool *they* prefer). When we do things like this we, organizationally, start to reek of bureaucratic stupidity. Suddenly every minor issue or annoyance is forced to fit into a bulky, unwieldy oversized "system." Then we start writing actions just so we can cross them off a list! Then before you know it your meetings start to be a dissection of open actions and never-ending new actions that are usually so mundane they shouldn't be an action on a list, they are the things most of us just do. But now, because of the system, we have to record and track and tic boxes and spend hours talking about things that good leaders just take care of. "Oh, did you put that in a 3 Legged 5 Why and get a list of countermeasures & containment plans from that truck company that delivered a non-critical item one day later than expected?!? Great, let me assign an action for you to close the other action." Then, people stop doing what they would normally have simply handled and "wait for a meeting and an action" to take care of it. Sludge, stagnation, delay, bureaucracy, over-processing…When you start attending meetings in which things aren't done because people were "waiting for the meeting" to discuss it, you're already losing ground on sense and sensibility. Go ahead, start looking for it at your next meeting.

Guess who is rejecting that? Gen Y & Z. They recognize it as a "Political, I'm Special and you are not" bias. Entire systems essentially get created from a personal agenda and then into a political platform. This bias does significant harm; especially in a super-managed super-systems super-metrics driven environments. Everything that is even slightly outside the system is viewed as a nail, and our system and "injector" employees become the hammer.

Force fitted constraining systems and methods are a sure-fire de-motivator and disconnecting, especially for those who recognize it when it is a political tool in workplace. Pure poison.

There are many unconscious biases and blind spots. Stereotypes, superiority, commitment bias, confirmation bias, in-group vs. out-group bias…again, once you start to try and learn what these biases are and start to look for them, I assure you, you will be stunned at their prevalence. Find them up front and start working on eliminating them, they are a disconnector.

To put a ribbon on this in the interests of keeping this pocket guide pocket sized- let us not forget about the obvious: Generational Bias. I don't know why, but I know it is: every generation thinks they are better than the generation before them and wiser than the generation after them. This particular bias really hit home with me at dinner with my family one evening. We were all sitting at the table, and the kids were talking to each other when I heard my 7th grade daughter tell her brothers that "her" generation is the last great generation and then she went on to start saying all the negative things in her mind about this "younger" generation…whom, by the way, were 5th

and 6th graders! I still laugh every time I have that memory; not only because it was my daughter (of course that is part of it) but mainly because I cannot think of a better single example of generational bias and the way it seems to be inherently wired into every single one of us.

I'm sure this may feel like, to the reader, I'm hammering hard on biases. There's a reason for it; it is critical to attracting, motivating and retaining Gen Y & Z. Not sure where to start looking, or what they are? Here's a short list of common & prevalent ones to dig into, as you are so inclined:

A few of my favorite unconscious Biases

Blind-spot bias – Our perception of reality is not influenced by biases. "My world view is perfect, I have absolutely no biases." Probably the biggest barrier to becoming unbiased because you don't look for your own.

Stereotypes – A well-known bias. You do it all the time. We make snap judgements and decisions based on gender, ethnicity, age, weight, clothes, etc.

Commitment Bias - Once we invest in something, we are less likely to let it go. Skilled negotiators utilize this to their advantage. If I'm buying a new car, I'll intentionally test drive 5 of them (even ones I'm not interested in). I'll have the salesman dig up mundane options and talk through all of them. I'll work that salesman for three or four hours, literally just for the sake of working them. Why? Towards the end, they are a lot more likely to negotiate price/options, whatever. They're committed to getting that sale they've just put so much work into.

Superiority Bias – You don't know what you don't know, but you think you do. You overestimate your strengths and underestimate your weaknesses. Careful here for when you get out of your depth on a topic. This is where I tell people in person that "fake it until you make it" is terrible advice that should be thrown directly into the trash where it belongs.

Contrast Bias – I've seen this most frequently on performance reviews again. Compare people to performance, not to the other employees.

Confirmation Bias - We embrace new information that confirms our original beliefs and reject information that contradicts. Perhaps unintentional, but either way we select and gravitate towards things that "agree with us."

Framing - Drawing different conclusions about the same piece of information depending on how or by whom it is presented. Ever had someone ask you to "go talk to so and so, because they won't listen to me but they will listen to you, even if we are saying the same things"? There you go.

Recency bias – We are doing a 12 month review, but all I can focus on and think about is the task you really screwed up (or hit a home run on) last week.

Egocentric Bias - Claiming to be solely or mainly responsible for a project or outcome that was a group effort. Many of us "type A" competitive, driven personalities have to learn to overcome this bias. You don't accomplish anything on your own, try to remember that.

The Field Does Not Come to the Farmer

6 TREAT THIS AS A PROCESS

If you've made it this far, and I hope you have, I strongly suspect you have noticed the narration style I have written in is not the typical style you get from books like these. This will be my last pro-tip for this reader: speak in common language. Do not use fancy, "headache" words that people have to look up to see what they mean. Part of leadership is getting our communication/vision into the mind of the receiver. When we use "headache" words to demonstrate how smart we are, we tend to lose part of our audience; and that is a direct failure.

As a Leader, I need to connect with people…so don't let your communication style get in the way of that connection. Keep it simple. Connect first in order to Attract and Impact.

Now, to pull together the prior 5 sections I need to instill the understanding in the reader that these things are all a process. My view is that attracting, motivating and retaining employees is a process; which means that I should view it as something with inputs, some process of transforming those inputs, and outputs. Consider it this way- if you manufactured some type of widget product, you would need raw materials (inputs), a machine to transform that raw material (process), and a finished widget that meets the specifications of the customer (outputs). We would surely put significant effort into establishing a good process before producing those finished widgets for our customers.

First, I would need to establish what the "finished product" specifications to be met are. What is a quality output, as dictated by the customer?

Second, I would need to establish what inputs I need in order to create the "finished product." What type of raw materials will work best? Where do I get those raw materials from? How many will I need at a time, and when will I need them? How will they be prepared, oriented, established, provided on time...

Third, I would need to consider all the potential failure modes and causes of variation that might occur during my process of transforming those raw materials (inputs) into those finished goods (outputs). I wouldn't simply buy a machine, plug it into the wall, turn it on and then start chucking raw materials at it and hope for the best, would I?

However, how often do we, as organizations, quite literally take that randomized approach at hiring, motivating and retaining employees? If I don't view fill rates, onboarding outputs with specifications, average length of service, turnover rates etc. as something that should be driven as a process then I am always going to be at the mercy of being driven by whatever results we are currently getting; based on nothing more than, honestly, hopes and dreams (therefore, usually disappointment).

A natural question here would be, "How do I start establishing a process for attracting, motivating and retaining employees?" I would recommend starting by taking a look at your existing systems, especially the failures as they have been. For example, when I hire a new employee and they quit in the first 30 days, I would try to brainstorm likely reasons they quit. A common (and good tool) to do something like this is a Cause & Effect diagram (also called a fishbone).

In the interests of staying in scope I shall give only a brief overview of how a Fishbone works; and also say that it is one tool of many available as a root cause analysis technique. A fishbone starts with an "effect" we want to dissect into potential causes. Typically this effect is some result we do not like or want, and want to avoid. In the following example, we list the undesired effect as "Gen Y & Z new hire quits."

Next, we consider all potential causes in our process that may result in this undesired output (effect). To help consider a greater set of scopes, we typically ask ourselves what causes exist in our process related to six categories (man, material, method, machine, measurement, environment) as shown in the following diagram. So I would consider why, for example, my new hire might have quit based on the People involved in our onboarding process? Then I would ask why that new hire may have quit based on the mechanics of my onboarding process? Then what about the methods of my onboarding process? The materials used to train in my onboarding process? The actual environment? The measurement system for good or bad in an onboarding process? What things might creep into my process that throw me off of my expected and desired output?

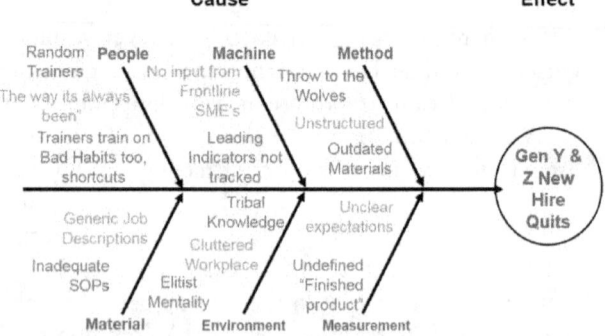

Cause and Effect, Ishakawa, or Fishbone, Diagram

Once I have put together a solid Fishbone Diagram that highlights potential variation causes, I can start to plan counter-measures or prevention measures to incorporate into my process to eliminate or minimize the odds of those variations to exist. The concept is simple; asking what can go wrong, and then planning ahead to ensure those things do not go wrong.

A useful tool for planning against variation is a Turtle Diagram. I like to start with my Output box for the process being considered. I want to start with the end in mind…asking, "What is a perfect actual product of this process?" If I don't define that first, I don't understand how I can complete the rest of the diagram or what am I actually driving to achieve? So, in our Output box in the following Turtle Diagram we have listed, "Properly Trained, Connected, Has a Growth Plan, Owner in the Process, and Autonomy on 3P's (people, planet, profit activities)."

From there I prefer to ask myself, "What inputs will I utilize to transform into the ideal Output?" and I complete the Input box.

Next I like to ask myself, "How will I use these inputs?" and I complete the How box.

From there I go to the What box. Here, I ask myself what I need and will utilize to get the items in my Input and How boxes?

Next I shift towards the Measure box. How will we know when we are winning or losing? How will we keep score as we test our plans and adjust? In our following example I listed things I would take an interest in. How much money does it cost when someone leaves? How many people are leaving within 30 days, 60 days, 90 days of being hired?

The last box I tend to fill out is the Who. For all these

boxes to successfully fall in line, who will we need to steer this program? I like to do this one last because far too frequently organizations start with "who" and that drives a weaker process. The Who box should be the starting point, so when planning, remember I want to start with the end in mind (Output box) and walk backwards through the system all the way to the beginning (Who box). When I take that approach, I tend to create a straighter, more intuitive flow than when I start at the beginning and try to push my through towards the end. Pushing from start to finish tends to create a hodge-podge, bending twisting turning process. It is best to start at the end, and pull the rest of the steps behind that to keep things straight and simple.

Turtle Diagram for Leading Gen Y & Z

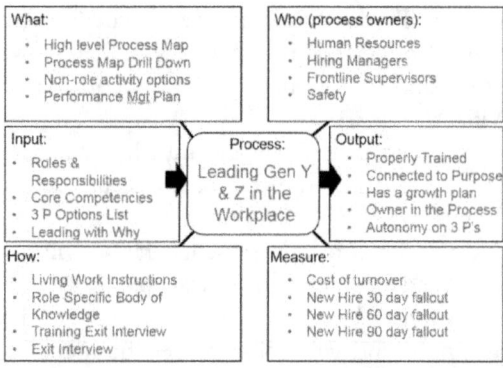

These two tools together (the Cause & Effect Diagram and the Turtle Diagram) are good starts for transforming an ad-hoc high effort loosely focused random result process into a more focused, output driven process that can be continuously improved.

7 EPILOGUE

Gen Y & Z are not only critical to your organizational success, they are powerful allies. Pass the torch with a clean hand-off and continue to let your legacy as a Leader flourish.

Remember, the Field Does not Come to the Farmer; rather, the Farmer must go to the Field to be successful.

The time to grow is now.

8 BIBLIOGRAPHY

Maslow's Hierarchy of Needs

Situational Leadership ***Image source:*** *Purdue MEP, Hersey, P., Blanchard, K. H., & Johnson, D. E. (2001). Management of organizational behavior: Leading human resources. Upper Saddle River, NJ: Prentice Hall.*

McClelland's Acquired Needs

A Method for Calculating Turnover Costs. Comcsystems.com Q4i Total Rewards. 2020.

Cause & Effect Diagram. Comcystems.com Q4i Total Rewards. 2020.

Turtle Diagram for Leading Gen Y & Z. Comcsystems.com Q4i Total Rewards. 2020.

9 ACKNOWLEDGEMENTS

Like all of us, I am a sum of my experiences. Many folks have directly and indirectly impacted my views. Some were positive impacts to build on, and some were negative impacts that gave me experiences "not to replicate." The marriage of the two types of experiences has allowed me to see linkages and interdependencies that have been tremendously beneficial to my career growth and, hopefully, the growth of the organizations I work with on a daily basis. In their efforts to be "bigger better faster safer smarter" the hope is that those achievements lead to a continuation of existing jobs as well as the creation of new jobs. We employ families, and that is not an insignificant concern. With that in mind, I want to acknowledge you, the reader for taking an interest in something that can directly benefit our workplaces and, therefore, our communities.

ABOUT THE AUTHOR

The author is a full-time instructor, trainer and consultant for the Purdue University Manufacturing Extension Partnership; primarily focused on Safety, Quality, Productivity and Leadership.

The author has achieved multiple certifications and awards, including the annual Purdue University MVP award for online Development and Instruction.

The author has been a frequent guest speaker at Leadership Camps and Public Workshops.

www.mep.purdue.edu

The author has worked extensively with leaders in multiple organizations across multiple industries; and is known (and commonly appreciated) for giving direct, common language advice based on real life experience; not answering questions with questions.

The author resides in Indiana and enjoys quiet time and early mornings. This is when everything is fresh, clear, focused and uninterrupted.

www.ingramcontent.com/pod-product-compliance
Lightning Source LLC
Chambersburg PA
CBHW070852220526
45466CB00005B/1964